Claim the
Benefits
of the Will

John Osteen

Unless otherwise indicated, all Scripture quotations in this book are from the King James Version of the Bible.

Lakewood Church
3700 SW Freeway
Houston, Texas 77027

www.lakewood.cc

ISBN 0–912631–03–1

CONTENTS

ONE

You Are Named in a Will

You could be rich and not even know it. In fact, if you are a Christian, you are! Did you know that you have received an inheritance? You are named in a will.

Just as a person draws up a Last Will and Testament so that when he or she dies, they leave an inheritance to persons they name in the will as heirs, God has drawn up His Last Will and Testament for His heirs. If you are a believer, you are an heir of God, and you have a right to claim the benefits of His Will. Romans 8:16-17 says, *The Spirit itself beareth witness with our spirit, that we are the children of God: and if children, then heirs; heirs of God, and joint-heirs with Christ.*

A will is not in force until the person who draws up the will, the testator, dies. There must be proof of the testator's death before the will becomes active. When the testator dies, the will is presented by the heirs for probate, whereby a competent judicial authority determines that the Last Will and Testament of the deceased person is genuine. If the will is contested, a lawyer and judge may be needed to settle the dispute. When the will is validated and you are named in the will as an heir, you have a right to claim the benefits left to you in that will.

The benefits of God's Will that we know as the Old Testament could only be claimed by people obeying the laws of God written in the law of Moses. If people disobeyed the law of God through sin, the people would be cursed instead of blessed because of their own disobedience. But God wanted His people blessed, so He gave them a sacrificial system whereby they would kill an animal and use its blood to substitute for the people to redeem them from the curse of the law and to atone for their sins. This blood only temporarily covered their sins from year to year — but God was writing another will! We call it the New Testament.

Matthew 26:26-28 tells us, *And as they were eating, Jesus took bread, and blessed it, and brake it, and gave it to the disciples, and said, Take, eat; this is my body. And he took the cup, and gave thanks, and gave it to them, saying, Drink ye all of it; for this is my blood of the **new testament**, which is shed for many for the remission of sins.* The word "testament" that is used in this scripture is the same word that we use for "will." Jesus was actually talking about His Last Will and Testament. A will is a legal document whereby a person states upon the event of his or her death that their possessions will be distributed to those named as heirs, as specified in the will. Upon the event of your own death, your will specifies that you give all the things you owned to certain individuals.

Your Bible is the will that God has given to the human race.

TWO

Jesus Is the Testator

But into the second [tabernacle] *went the high priest alone once every year, not without blood*, *which he offered for himself, and for the errors of the people: the Holy Ghost this signifying, that the way into the holiest of all was not yet made manifest, while as the first tabernacle was yet standing: which was a figure for the time then present, in which were offered both gifts and sacrifices, that could not make him that did the service perfect, as pertaining to the conscience.*

*Neither by the blood of goats and calves, **but by his own blood he entered in once into the*** *holy place*, *having obtained eternal redemption for us.*

How much more shall **the blood of Christ, who through the eternal Spirit offered himself** *without spot to God, purge your conscience from dead works to serve the Living God? And for this cause he is the mediator of the new testament, that by means of death, for the redemption of the transgressions that were under the first testament, they which are called might receive the promise of eternal inheritance* (Hebrews 9:7-9,12,14-15).

This passage makes it clear that Jesus Christ is the mediator of the New Testament. He is the One who not only left us His Will, but because He ever lives to make intercession for us, He will see that His Will is enforced! Jesus is our Great High Priest seated at the right hand of the Father to guarantee that we receive everything He has promised us in the Bible.

Hebrews 9:16-17 tells us, ***For where a testament is, there must also of necessity be the death of the testator.*** *For a testament is of force after men are dead otherwise it is of no strength at all while the testator liveth.*

A Will is Valid Only After a Death

You see, there must be a death before a will becomes valid.

The Old Testament was ratified under the law of Moses with the blood of animals that died as substitutes for the people's sins (see Hebrews 9:20,22). But God promised a New Testament, or Will, that would eradicate all sin so the benefits of God could be enjoyed by all those who are in covenant with Him.

Hebrews 10:16-23 says, *This is the covenant* (will) *that I will make with them after those days, saith the Lord, I will put My laws into their hearts, and in their minds will I write them; and their sins and iniquities will I remember no more. Now where remission of these is, there is no more offering for sin.* **Having therefore, brethren, boldness to enter into the holiest by the blood of Jesus**, *by a new and living way, which he hath consecrated for us, through the veil, that is to say, his flesh; and having an high priest over the house of God; let us draw near with a true heart in full assurance of faith, having our hearts sprinkled from an evil conscience, and our bodies washed with pure water, Let us hold fast the profession of our faith without wavering; (for* **he is faithful that promised***).*

In this New Testament, God's Will was

ratified not with the blood of animals, but with the precious blood of His Son, Jesus Christ.

God left you and me something in His Will. You ask, "Where is the Will?" It is in your Bible. That is God's Will!

The Will that God wrote defines all the benefits that belong to every individual mentioned in His Will. That is one reason you need to read your Bible. Jesus died, but He left us His Will. In the Will, God has recorded what Jesus, through His death, purchased for you and me.

The story is told of a Christian on his way to an underground church meeting many years ago in one of the "iron curtain" countries. Of course, Christian meetings were forbidden, and the meetings were held in secret. This Christian was stopped by the police and questioned as to where he was going at that time of night. The Christian would never think of lying, so he silently stood, waiting for the wisdom of the Holy Ghost to give him an answer. When the answer came, he looked at the policeman and said very calmly, "My Elder Brother has died, and we in the family are gathering together tonight to read and discuss His Will in order that we may know what He has left us." This satisfied the policeman, and the Christian was allowed to go on his way.

Of course, what the Christian meant was that Jesus, our Elder Brother, had died as the Lamb of God for our redemption, and that he was going to a meeting of Christians (the family of God) to open the Word of God, which is the Will of God. There they would discuss and rejoice in what the Lord Jesus Christ had promised them in this wonderful Will, which is the Word of God!

THREE

The Blood of Jesus Is Proof of His Death

As I mentioned earlier, a will is only in force after the testator dies. Once he dies, the will must be probated. In order to probate the will, there has to be proof of the death. **This is why the blood of Jesus is so important.** Jesus did not leave one drop of His blood here on earth. When He shed His blood on Calvary and then appeared to Mary Magdalene, He told her, *Touch me not; for I am not yet ascended to my Father* (John 20:17).

11

Later, when Jesus appeared to the disciples, He said in Luke 24:39, *Behold my hands and my feet, that it is I myself: **handle me**, and see; for a spirit hath not flesh and bones, as ye see me have.*

Jesus told Mary Magdalene, "Don't touch Me." Then He told His disciples, "Handle Me." Between these two incidents, Jesus had ascended to the Father. He took every drop of His precious blood into the Holiest of Holies in the heavenly sanctuary. The book of Hebrews tells us that **Jesus' blood is sprinkled before the mercy seat of God as evidence that Jesus actually died!**

Hebrews 9:24 says, *For Christ is not entered into the holy places made with hands, which are the figures of the true; but into heaven itself, now to appear in the presence of God for us.*

Revelation 12:11 tells us, *And they overcame him* (the devil) *by the blood of the Lamb, and by the word of their testimony; and they loved not their lives unto the death.*

Leviticus 17:11 says, *The life of the flesh is in the blood.*

When Jesus took His blood before the Father, that blood settled forever that He had died. The angels know it. Demons know it. The devil knows it. The Father knows it. Jesus had come to earth and actually gone through death in a physical body. Then He took His blood to heaven and sprinkled it at the mercy seat of God, the Father.

Hebrews 12:22-24 states, *But ye are come unto Mount Zion, and unto the city of the living God, the heavenly Jerusalem, and to an innumerable company of angels, to the general assembly and church of the firstborn, which are written in heaven, and to God the Judge of all, and to the spirits of just men made perfect, and to Jesus the mediator of the new covenant,* **and to the BLOOD of sprinkling,** *that speaketh better things than that of Abel.*

When you get to heaven, that blood will still be there. That blood is evidence that Jesus died and that His Will is in effect! You need to be sure that you know God's Will is operating for you NOW. This will help you in fighting the battles of life.

A will is of no effect until someone dies. Your own will is worthless to your heirs until you die. It will not give another person one thing until you die.

The blood that Jesus shed is in heaven as evidence that He did die. What He left us in the Bible is absolutely and justifiably ours in the sight of God, in the sight of the devil, and in the sight of man.

FOUR

You Must Read the Will Before You Can Claim Your Benefits

Did you know that in this land and in other lands there are millions and millions of dollars' worth of unclaimed, will benefits that heirs know nothing about? Some courts, not knowing what to do with it, finally just give it to the state. Some people have never been told that they were named in a will. Some people know they are mentioned, but they have never taken the time to investigate what their inheritance might be.

Some people are rich because of God's Will and do not even know it! There is an abundance on deposit in their name, and the Will says it belongs to them — yet they do not have it. Many of them know nothing about it because they have never been told they have had an inheritance given to them.

Several years ago, I was conducting a meeting in Tulsa, Oklahoma, preaching the Good News and praying for the sick every night. One evening as I was having supper in a restaurant, I noticed a crippled woman being seated at a table near me. She laid her crutches down, and with great difficulty, finally got seated for her meal.

Compassion rose up within me for this woman, so I went over and introduced myself and told her why I was in the city. Then I explained in detail God's promises regarding healing. I shared about the healing of our daughter Lisa, who was born with a disease similar to cerebral palsy, but who was healed by the Lord Jesus Christ. (You can read the complete story of Lisa's healing in my book, *There is a Miracle in Your Mouth*.)

I shared several instances of God's great mercy in healing. When I finished, she said, "Why, Brother Osteen, if Jesus wants me to suffer like this, I am perfectly willing to suffer for Him. I have no complaints. I am happy to suffer on His behalf."

In spite of all I could say in trying to explain to her God's Will, she was completely convinced that she was "suffering for Jesus." I knew that she would go to her grave in that crippled condition because she would not listen to what Jesus had left her in His Will.

That very same night, as I preached to the people at my meeting, I explained what God had left us in His Will regarding healing and miracles. A pastor suddenly rushed to the platform, bringing a child. He said, "This child goes to our church. He has had a club foot all of his life, but while you were teaching, suddenly it straightened out and became perfectly normal."

What a difference in the two people! The woman would not accept what the Will said, and she remained crippled. However, as I read the Will that said healing belonged to the little boy, he simply believed, in child-like faith, and instantly he was made whole!

We need to know what is ours as stated in the Will that God has given us. We need to read the Will every day and find out what is in it. We need to find out what God has left us! Many people are living as paupers because they do not know that God has provided in His will a way for them to be spiritually rich, physically rich and financially rich.

But benefits must be known before they can be claimed! You cannot claim anything that the Bible states is yours until you know about it. This is the reason you need to read your Will — the Bible — every day.

It is a wonderful revelation to find out what Jesus did for us and what He has left for us!

Someone Read the Will to Me

I can well remember when I was not a Christian. I was lost. I served myself and Satan. I lived in the realm of worldly things, and it was displeasing to God. I was dead spiritually. I had no interest in the things of God, and I knew nothing about the Will that He had left for me. I was ignorant of what was mine through Jesus' death, burial and resurrection.

One day, when I did not know a thing in the world about His Will, my high school friend, Sam Martin read me a part of it. He showed me that the Will said, *For God so loved the world, that he gave his only begotten Son, that whosoever* (that included me) *believeth in him should not perish, but have everlasting life* (John 3:16).

I discovered that I was included in a will. I was included in God's Will, the Will of the Lord Jesus Christ! He had left me something called *everlasting life!*

I found out that the Will said, *But as many as received him, to them gave he power to become the **sons of God*** (John 1:12).

God promised, *He that believeth on the Son hath everlasting life: and he that believeth not the Son shall not see life; but the wrath of God abideth on him* (John 3:36).

Jesus said, *Verily, verily, I say unto you, He that heareth my word* (My Will)*, and believeth on him that sent me, hath everlasting life, and shall not come into condemnation; but is passed from death unto life* (John 5:24).

Then I read how to claim this benefit of eternal life. Romans 10:9-10 says, *If thou shalt confess with thy mouth the Lord Jesus, and shalt believe in thine heart that God hath raised him from the dead, thou shalt be saved. For with the heart man believeth unto righteousness; and with the mouth confession is made unto salvation.*

I found out that if I would open my heart, Jesus would come into my heart and save me. I discovered that if I confessed Him as my Lord, I would pass from spiritual death into eternal life. I found that I could be relieved of the burden of my sins. I learned that I could be an heir of God and a joint-heir with Jesus Christ. That sounded good – and since Jesus died and left me His Will, I decided to claim it!

I opened my heart and asked Jesus to come in. I claimed and confessed Him as my Lord on July 30, 1939. I became a Christian on that very day because I found out I was mentioned in His Will.

Do you know that you are mentioned in God's Will?

He left us so much. There is **so much!**

He left us His Name!

He left us power over demons!

He left us the Holy Ghost!

He left us innumerable blessings through His death, burial and resurrection. When He died, He left us everything the Father had given to Him. Everything we have been given is all written down. Every day we should get out the Will and check it to see what else God has left us.

When you find something in the Will that you need, take the blood of Jesus Christ and say, "Father, I found this in the Will. I ask You to open up the rich treasury of heaven and give me what belongs to me. Today, I discovered that it is mine!

"The blood of Jesus is sprinkled in heaven as proof that He died for me. The blood of Jesus says I have a right to my inheritance, so I come boldly to Your throne of grace to claim what rightfully belongs to me."

I Had To Check the Will

I remember one time when the devil attacked my physical body. He wanted to kill

19

me. He would like to kill all of us.

During that dark time in my life, I began to check the Will. I thought, "I need to check the Will to see if God has anything to say about this situation."

We should check out every situation with the Word of God first.

I began to check the Will, and I found out in Matthew 8:17 that Jesus took my infirmities on Himself and bore my sicknesses.

I discovered in the Will — in 1 Peter 2:24 — that it says, (Jesus) *his own self bare our sins in his own body on the tree, that we, being dead to sins, should live unto righteousness: by whose stripes ye **were** healed.*

God told me in Exodus 15:26, *I am the Lord that healeth thee.*

These promises were written to me, so I searched further in the Will.

Mark 16:18 says, *They shall lay hands on the sick, and they **shall** recover.*

I read in the Will, *Is any sick among you? Let him call for the elders of the church; and let them pray over him, anointing him with oil in the name of the Lord: and the prayer of faith **shall** save the sick, and the Lord **shall** raise him up* (James 5:14-15).

Then one day I found something great in the Will. Galatians 3:13 says, *Christ hath redeemed us from the curse of the law, being made a curse for us: for it is written, Cursed is every one that hangeth on a tree.*

I discovered "the curse of the law" in Deuteronomy, chapter 28. I found that there was every kind of sickness in the curse of the law. The sicknesses named were consumption, fever, inflammation and extreme burning (verse 22); and botch, emerods, scab, itch, madness, blindness and astonishment of heart (verse 27).

Then in Deuteronomy 28:60-61 it says, *Moreover he will bring upon thee all the diseases of Egypt, which thou wast afraid of; and they shall cleave unto thee. Also **every sickness, and every plague, which is not written in the book of this law**, them will the Lord bring upon thee, until thou be destroyed.*

What an amazing discovery! Every sickness and plague — even those not named in the Bible — are a part of the curse of the law! But the Will says in Galatians 3:13 that *"**Christ hath redeemed (me)** from the curse of the law."* I was actually redeemed from all sickness and disease — ALL!

The Will said the redemption price was the blood of Jesus. *Forasmuch as ye know that ye were not redeemed with corruptible things, as silver and gold, from your vain conversation received by tradition from your fathers; but with the precious blood of Christ, as of a lamb without blemish and without spot* (1 Peter 1:18-19).

The Holy Ghost confirmed this in my own spirit and said, "God bought you – spirit, soul and body. You are redeemed. These scriptures list your benefits."

Now, you can leave your benefits unclaimed if you want to, but I decided to claim mine!

Deep inside of me, my spirit began to say, "I believe I will go and knock on the door of heaven and claim my benefits."

So I claimed my benefits that very day. By the time the sun was hot on the earth, I had claimed my benefits in the high court of heaven. God healed my body from the top of my head to the bottom of my feet. The benefits of His Will were mine! They had been mine all the time — but they did me no good until I found them and claimed them personally. Several years have passed, and even though the devil has tried to attack my body again, I still walk in divine health!

Some people have never touched the Will. They have never opened the Will, so they do not know what they are missing. If they would take time to read it, they would find out that they don't have to be poor, barely "getting by" in life. They would discover that they don't have to be sickly all the time, just dragging through life defeated and depressed.

Check the Will! Find out what God left you through the death, burial and resurrection of the Lord Jesus Christ.

I like what I call "The Ten Club Plan" for daily Bible reading. With this plan, you read ten chapters every day — two in the Old Testament, two in the New Testament, five Psalms, and one Proverb. This will take you through the Old Testament one time per year, through the New Testament more than three times a year, and through the books of praise and wisdom monthly.

Every day you should read the New Testament. Read it over and over and over again. I have been reading it for more than 55 years, and I am still finding new things I never saw in all my life. It is wonderful to read the Will!

FIVE

A Will Can Be Contested

Did you know that a will can be contested?

Every time you try to claim anything from God, the devil will contest that Will. He will come to you and say, "No, that is not right. That promise is not for you —that was just for the apostles. That was for somebody else. You had better be careful about taking God at His Word literally. You may die."

That is the voice of the enemy, and it is a lie!

I read the story of a young lady who told how learning that she was named in the Will changed her life with a miracle of healing. Below are the young lady's own words, recounting her testimony:

When I was born, it was soon to be discovered that I would face death at an early age. My diagnosis came at 1½ years of age. The doctors said I was born with an incurable, hereditary disease called Cystic Fibrosis. My life span at the most would be 18 years.

As time went along, new discoveries were made to help prolong my life

to reach the eighteen-year span; but, even to this day, no medical cure has been found. This disease is the "killer" amongst children.

I began school at six years, taking with me the enzyme pills that were necessary to digest my food at every meal because of my non-functioning pancreas. This was a big responsibility for a child of that age to remember to do.

By the time I was ten, respirators were introduced into my life. Breathing was a continuous struggle. Several times I almost choked to death on the excessive amount of mucus produced in my lungs.

Strong antibiotics became a daily part of my life. More and more, my life was becoming dependent upon doctors, machines, hospitals and medication.

My early teens began with a "bang" of new additions to my "survival kit." Physical therapy treatments three times a day, along with more powerful respirators and "mist tents" (oxygen tents with medication blowing in continually) became a part of my daily routine. Nothing would sustain my deteriorating body. Even the common cold meant hospitalization for me.

By the time I was sixteen years of age, I weighed sixty-nine pounds, with part of one lung collapsed, only 5% good fibrous tissues left to breathe with, and high temperatures that sometimes took months to subdue. The doctors said they had done all that they could do for me. I might live about a year if I did not have any more colds, for that is what started the frightening fever on the rise again.

Now I was about a year away from that early point of death that I had been taught about and prepared to face all of my life. I had accepted Jesus as my Lord and Savior when I was fourteen. I was a member of the Church of Christ at that time.

I knew without a shadow of a doubt that I would go to heaven when I died, but I could not see death as a part of God's plan for my life at this time. Circumstances looked impossible, but with God all things are possible (see Mark 10:27).

I heard about and began attending a home prayer meeting in my hometown where I received the Baptism in the

Holy Spirit. This made an open channel for God to begin teaching me His Will and His ways. I read in Matthew 8:17, Himself took our infirmities, and bare our sicknesses. The Lord showed me that Jesus bore our sicknesses on the cross just like He bore our sins. I knew then that I would not die, but live, and declare the works of God.

After two months of learning what God's Word had to say about healing, the Lord spoke to me and said, "I am going to heal you." Praise the Lord! Every night for the past year I had prayed that the Lord would help someone find a cure for Cystic Fibrosis. This was beyond my fondest dreams! God wanted to heal me and receive all the glory Himself.

A week or two later the Lord spoke again, saying, "I am going to heal you tomorrow night." The excitement was so great I could hardly wait! I did not know what to expect. I had never known the Lord to do these things before. But still I did not question how or doubt that I would be healed. I was naive enough to believe that God meant what He said.

The next night at the prayer meeting,

the Lord gave His final Word, "Now is the time. I am ready to heal you. You have waited long enough." So I asked for prayer for healing, and the Lord miraculously healed me. The warmth of God's healing hand began in my pancreas. It released all the mucus that had prevented its functioning all my life. This divine warmth moved through my lungs and cleared them as it went. For the first time in my life, I knew what it was like to take a deep breath of fresh air. From that night forward, I discontinued all medication. [NOTE: *We do not recommend that any person stop taking medication a doctor has prescribed. This young woman chose to do this of her own volition.*]

On that day, September 13, 1971, at the age of seventeen, I began a new life totally for the Lord. I was a normal, human being.

The Lord began teaching me a lot concerning healing and confession. For a few days everything was glorious. Then came the reality of what Jesus said in John 10:10, *The thief cometh not, but for to steal, and to kill, and to destroy: I am come that they might have life, and that they might have it more abundantly.*

The devil always contests what Jesus has given, but I had found out about my benefits in the Will of God. The devil was trying to "contest the will."

EVERY SYMPTOM OF CYSTIC FIBROSIS CAME UPON ME, INCLUDING SYMPTOMS OF A COLLAPSED LUNG. THE DEVIL TRIED TO STEAL WHAT GOD HAD GIVEN ME. IT WAS MY CHOICE TO HANG ON TO GOD AND CONFESS GOD'S WORD, OR TO SAY, "OH, I WAS NOT HEALED."

Proverbs 18:21 says, *Death and life are in the power of the tongue.* In my case, this was literally true. So I began confessing God's Word continually that "by Jesus' stripes I am healed." After a week, the battle ended. JESUS WAS THE VICTOR. I NOW HAD THAT ABUNDANT LIFE THAT JESUS PROMISED ME.

Two months later, I went back to my doctor to have the healing verified. I told him what had happened. He asked, "Have you been to a faith healer?" I answered, "Well, there is only one healer, and that is Jesus Christ." He ran tests and made x-rays of my lungs. When he listened to my lungs, he said they were perfectly clear. He compared the x-rays with all the previous ones only to find healthy lungs. The only thing present on the x-rays was my cross pendant that had fallen down over the lung that had been collapsed. The doctor wrote at the end of my chart, "COMPLETELY FREE OF CYSTIC FIBROSIS."

What a wonderful testimony! Let me tell you — if there is a devil, there is a Jesus! If there is a devil, there is certainly a God. When the devil comes to harass you, remind yourself that if there is a devil, there is also a God. Most people know the devil is out there. But, friend, GOD IS THERE ALSO. Jesus is real!

There is a God who spoke this world into existence. He has a Son named Jesus who died for you and rose again. You have many legal rights in His Will.

Read Your Rights to the Devil
The devil will contest the Will. He will try to contest the Will every time you take a promise from it. Do you know what I do

when he tries to put a symptom on me or come against me in other ways? I do not stare at what the old devil is doing. I say, "Wait a minute, ol' devil. Let me just check the Will. Let me see if it has changed any. I am going to read it to you, Mr. Devil, just in case you haven't read it. Look, Galatians 3:13 still says *Christ hath redeemed* (me) *from the curse of the law.* Now, Devil, since you are contesting this Will, let's look at Deuteronomy 28. It says that all sickness is a curse of the law; therefore, the Will says I am redeemed from the curse of the law and sickness cannot be a part of me!" The devil will **flee** before God's Word.

The Bible says in Revelation 12:11, *They overcame him* (the devil) *by the blood of the Lamb, and by the word of their testimony; and they loved not their lives unto the death.*

You must trust your life to God. You overcome the devil by the blood of Jesus and by the word of your testimony. You have the Will. You have the Blood. You have God's Will and the proof that Jesus died to make His Will effective. All you have to do is claim the blood of Jesus Christ at the throne of God. Quote from some of the Will and declare that it is yours! Then act like it. Yes, I say, dare to act like the benefits of God's Will are yours!

Act like it, even though, you don't feel like it. Faith requires action! Then hold fast to your confession of deliverance when the devil tries to steal your benefits.

SIX

You Have a Lawyer

When the Will is contested, you have a lawyer. The Bible says in 1 John 2:1-2, *My little children, these things write I unto you, that ye sin not. And if any man sin, we have an advocate* [lawyer] *with the Father, Jesus Christ the righteous: and he is the propitiation for our sins: and not for ours only, but also for the sins of the whole world.*

In a court where a will is probated, there is a lawyer and a judge who make sure that the heirs receive the benefits of the will that legally belong to them. In the high court of heaven, we have Jesus as our Lawyer, and our Heavenly Father is the Judge. You just cannot lose with a team like that!

When the devil begins to contest the Will, trying to accuse you and rob you, your Lawyer stands to defend you. The Judge sits on the bench, and your Lawyer begins by saying, "I just want you to look, Father, at My hands. Look at My feet and My side. Behold, I am the One that died. My blood is sprinkled here before You as proof of My purchasing their benefits. The Will is in effect!"

The Book of Revelation says that He was as a lamb slain. With His precious hand, He points to His blood and says, "Father, look upon that blood that I shed in My human body to purchase the benefits for My children. I declare that the devil's objection is nullified, and they have the benefits that I purchased for them."

We have a Lawyer...and His name is Jesus. When the Will is contested, He stands and fights our case to give us the victory!

You Must Read and Confess the Will

We must learn to check the Will. We need to know what we have. Most people lose their fight when the will is being contested because they do not have any assurance of what they really have.

I remember an incident that happened one day while walking my dog, Scooter. Every day, Scooter and I would walk to the end of our street, past the corner house where a cat lived. Every day, Scooter would

33

run after that cat and chase him up a tree. This happened every day, day after day. Every day, Scooter would run that cat up a tree. I thought to myself, "It looks like that cat would get tired of being chased and just stay up in the tree because he knows Scooter is going to come after him. Scooter is going to catch him one day."

On this particular day, however, it all changed. To my amazement, when Scooter began to chase the cat, the cat stood his ground, bowed his back and bared his claws. Just when I thought the cat would be dead in a few more seconds, Scooter took a sharp turn and avoided the confrontation altogether. Scooter actually ran from the cat! That cat had had enough, and he stood up to Scooter. (I think that cat had been going to Lakewood Church!) That's the way we need to treat the devil when he contests God's Will for our lives. Scooter never contested that cat again from the day the cat stood up to his harassment. When you get tired of the devil's harassment, you will have victory, too!

This is why you need to read the Word of God and be familiar with your benefits. You need to claim those benefits and keep your confession in line with the Word. Keep on saying what you have in God. Keep your stand in faith strong. When the devil begins to contest you, know that you have the victory because the blood of the Lord Jesus Christ and the Word of God says you do!

Your physical body may seem sick, but the Bible says, *With his stripes we are healed* (Isaiah 53:5).

Keep Your Eyes on Your Inheritance

The Bible says in Romans 4:20-21 that Abraham did not consider his own body, which was past the age of childbearing when God promised him a son. *He staggered not at the promise of God through unbelief; but was strong in faith, giving glory to God; and being fully persuaded that, what he had promised, he was able also to perform.* He kept his eyes on what God had said to him.

When Abraham kept his eyes on what God had said to him, then God made it effective, and he became known as the *friend of God* (James 2:23).

First John 5:14-15 says, *And this is the confidence that we have in him, that, if we ask any thing according to his will, he heareth us: and if we know that he hear us, whatsoever we ask, we know that we have the petitions that we desired of him.*

In Jeremiah 1:12 (The Amplified Bible), the Lord says, *I am…watching over My word to perform it.*

Let me encourage you to check the Will every day. When it seems like everything is going wrong, open that Will God left you. The Bible says, "Let not these promises depart from your eyes" (see Proverbs 4:21). Let your physical eyes look on what the Will says.

When the devil begins to harass you, don't just call the scripture to remembrance in your mind (although that is helpful, too). Don't let God's Word depart from your eyes. Go get the Will and open it up and read it. Joshua 1:8 says, *This book of the law shall not depart out of thy mouth; but thou shalt meditate therein day and night, that thou mayest observe to do according to all that is written therein: for then thou shalt make thy way prosperous, and then thou shalt have good success.* Read the Will ALOUD and declare your rights according to the Will.

Some people begin to cry when the devil attacks them. They moan and groan and begin to look for a minister somewhere to come to their rescue.

NO! NO! NO!

GO READ THE WILL!

Learn to stand on the Word of God yourself. Learn to grow up in God. Learn to find out what God left you in Christ. Learn to know who you are in God.

Boldly take the promise in the Will to the Father and say, "Father, here is Your promise to me. I refuse to continue in this problem. No demon is going to harass me. I am not going to live in poverty spiritually, financially or physically. I am claiming my benefits in the Lord Jesus Christ for me and my household. The blood of Jesus is the basis of my claim. That shows that He died for me, and He arose again to mediate this Will. I am claiming it. I will not let the devil rob me."

It is such a joy to have something to read every day that will undergird us and strengthen us in the things that God wants us to have!

Knock on the door of heaven and claim everything that belongs to you. Carefully study the Will. Read it and claim your benefits. Once you have claimed it, HOLD IT FAST! Do not let the devil rob you. The blood of Jesus Christ is your surety for everything for which He died.

Learn what is in the Will and begin to act on it. You will find that you are rich in God! A limitless inheritance is YOURS!

SEVEN

The Benefits in the Will That Belong to You

Salvation

Mark 8:35 *For whosoever will save his life shall lose it; but whosoever shall lose his life for my sake and the gospel's, the same shall save it.*

John 1:12 *But as many as received him, to them gave he power to become the sons of God, even to them that believe on his name.*

John 1:29 *The next day John seeth Jesus coming unto him, and saith, Behold the Lamb of God, which taketh away the sin of the world.*

John 3:3 *Jesus answered and said unto him, Verily, verily, I say unto thee, Except a man be born again, he cannot see the kingdom of God.*

John 3:16-17 *For God so loved the world, that he gave his only begotten Son, that whosoever believeth in him should not perish, but have everlasting life. For God sent not his Son into the world to condemn the world; but that the world through him might be saved.*

John 3:36 *He that believeth on the Son hath everlasting life: and he that believeth not the Son shall not see life; but the wrath of God abideth on him.*

Acts 2:21 *And it shall come to pass, that whosoever shall call on the name of the Lord shall be saved.*

Acts 3:19 *Repent ye therefore, and be converted, that your sins may be blotted out, when the times of refreshing shall come from the presence of the Lord.*

Acts 4:12 *Neither is there salvation in any other: for there is none other name under heaven given among men, whereby we must be saved.*

Acts 10:43 *To him give all the prophets witness, that through his name whosoever believeth in him shall receive remission of sins.*

Acts 16:30-31 *And brought them out, and said, Sirs, what must I do to be saved? And they said,*

Believe on the Lord Jesus Christ, and thou shalt be saved, and thy house.

Romans 3:23-24 *For all have sinned, and come short of the glory of God; being justified freely by his grace through the redemption that is in Christ Jesus.*

Romans 5:6 *For when we were yet without strength, in due time Christ died for the ungodly.*

Romans 6:23 *For the wages of sin is death; but the gift of God is eternal life through Jesus Christ our Lord.*

Romans 10:9-10 *That if thou shalt confess with thy mouth the Lord Jesus, and shalt believe in thine heart that God hath raised him from the dead, thou shalt be saved. For with the heart man believeth unto righteousness; and with the mouth confession is made unto salvation.*

2 Corinthians 5:17 *Therefore if any man be in Christ, he is a new creature: old things are passed away; behold, all things are become new.*

Ephesians 2:8 *For by grace are ye saved through faith; and that not of yourselves: it is the gift of God.*

1 Peter 2:24 *Who his own self bare our sins in his own body on the tree, that we, being dead to sins, should live unto righteousness: by whose stripes ye were healed.*

1 John 5:11-13 *And this is the record, that God hath given to us eternal life, and this life is in his Son. He that hath the Son hath life; and he that hath not the Son of God hath not life. These things have I written unto you that believe on the name of the Son of God; that ye may know that ye have eternal life, and that ye may believe on the name of the Son of God.*

The Baptism in the Holy Ghost

Isaiah 28:11 *For with stammering lips and another tongue will he speak to this people.*

Joel 2:28 *And it shall come to pass afterward, that I will pour out my spirit upon all flesh; and your sons and your daughters shall prophesy, your old men shall dream dreams, your young men shall see visions.*

Matthew 3:11 *I indeed baptize you with water unto repentance: but he that cometh after me is mightier than I, whose shoes I am not worthy to* *bear: he shall baptize you with the Holy Ghost, and with fire.*

Mark 16:17 *And these signs shall follow them that believe; in my name shall they cast out devils; they shall speak with new tongues.*

Luke 3:22 *And the Holy Ghost descended in a bodily shape like a dove upon him, and a voice came from heaven, which said, Thou art my beloved Son; in thee I am well pleased.*

Luke 11:13 *If ye then, being evil, know how to give good gifts unto your children: how much more shall your heavenly Father give the Holy Spirit to them that ask him?*

Luke 24:49 *And, behold, I send the promise of my Father upon you: but tarry ye in the city of Jerusalem, until ye be endued with power from on high.*

John 14:26 *But the Comforter, which is the Holy Ghost, whom the Father will send in my name, he shall teach you all things, and bring all things to your remembrance, whatsoever I have said unto you.*

Acts 1:4 *And, being assembled together with them, commanded them that they should not depart from Jerusalem, but wait for the promise of the Father, which, saith he, ye have heard of me.*

Acts 1:5 *For John truly baptized with water; but ye shall be baptized with the Holy Ghost not many days hence.*

Acts 1:8 *But ye shall receive power, after that the Holy Ghost is come upon you: and ye shall be witnesses unto me both in Jerusalem, and in all Judaea, and in Samaria, and unto the uttermost part of the earth.*

Acts 2:4 *And they were all filled with the Holy Ghost, and began to speak with other tongues, as the Spirit gave them utterance.*

Acts 2:38-39 *Then Peter said unto them, Repent, and be baptized every one of you in the name of Jesus Christ for the remission of sins, and ye shall receive the gift of the Holy Ghost. For the promise is unto you, and to your children, and to all that are afar off, even as many as the Lord our God shall call.*

Acts 5:32 *And we are his witnesses of these things; and so is also the Holy Ghost, whom God hath given to them that obey him.*

Acts 19:6 *And when Paul had laid his hands upon them, the Holy Ghost came on them; and they spake with tongues, and prophesied.*

Romans 8:26 *Likewise the Spirit also helpeth our infirmities: for we know not what we should pray for as we ought: but the Spirit itself maketh intercession for us with groanings which cannot be uttered.*

1 Corinthians 14:2 *For he that speaketh in an unknown tongue speaketh not unto men, but unto God: for no man understandeth him; howbeit in the spirit he speaketh mysteries.*

1 Corinthians 14:15 *What is it then? I will pray with the spirit, and I will pray with the understanding also: I will sing with the spirit, and I will sing with the understanding also.*

1 Corinthians 14:39 *Wherefore, brethren, covet to prophesy, and forbid not to speak with tongues.*

Ephesians 6:18 *Praying always with all prayer*

and supplication in the Spirit, and watching thereunto with all perseverance and supplication for all saints.

Jude 1:20 *But ye, beloved, building up yourselves on your most holy faith, praying in the Holy Ghost.*

Healing

Exodus 15:26 *And said, If thou wilt diligently hearken to the voice of the Lord thy God, and wilt do that which is right in his sight, and wilt give ear to his commandments, and keep all his statutes, I will put none of these diseases upon thee, which I have brought upon the Egyptians: for I am the Lord that healeth thee.*

Exodus 23:25 *And ye shall serve the Lord your God, and he shall bless thy bread, and thy water; and I will take sickness away from the midst of thee.*

Psalm 91:16 *With long life will I satisfy him, and shew him my salvation.*

Psalm 103:3 *Who forgiveth all thine iniquities; who healeth all thy diseases.*

45

Psalm 107:20 *He sent his word, and healed them, and delivered them from their destructions.*

Psalm 118:17 *I shall not die, but live, and declare the works of the Lord.*

Proverbs 4:20-22 *My son, attend to my words; incline thine ear unto my sayings. Let them not depart from thine eyes; keep them in the midst of thine heart. For they are life unto those that find them, and health to all their flesh.*

Proverbs 17:22 *A merry heart doeth good like a medicine: but a broken spirit drieth the bones.*

Isaiah 53:5 *But he was wounded for our transgressions, he was bruised for our iniquities: the chastisement of our peace was upon him; and with his stripes we are healed.*

Jeremiah 30:17 *For I will restore health unto thee, and I will heal thee of thy wounds, saith the Lord.*

Joel 3:10 *Beat your plowshares into swords and your pruning hooks into spears: let the weak say, I am strong.*

Malachi 4:2 *But unto you that fear my name shall the Sun of righteousness arise with healing in his wings; and ye shall go forth, and grow up as calves of the stall.*

Matthew 4:23 *And Jesus went about all Galilee, teaching in their synagogues, and preaching the gospel of the kingdom, and healing all manner of sickness and all manner of disease among the people.*

Matthew 8:17 *That it might be fulfilled which was spoken by Esaias the prophet, saying, Himself took our infirmities, and bare our sicknesses.*

Mark 16:18 *They shall take up serpents; and if they drink any deadly thing, it shall not hurt them; they shall lay hands on the sick, and they shall recover.*

Luke 1:37 *For with God nothing shall be impossible.*

Luke 9:6 *And they departed, and went through the towns, preaching the gospel, and healing every where.*

John 14:14 *If ye shall ask any thing in my name, I will do it.*

Acts 5:16 *There came also a multitude out of the cities round about unto Jerusalem, bringing sick folks, and them which were vexed with unclean spirits: and they were healed every one.*

Acts 10:38 *How God anointed Jesus of Nazareth with the Holy Ghost and with power: who went about doing good, and healing all that were oppressed of the devil; for God was with him.*

Romans 8:2 *For the law of the Spirit of life in Christ Jesus hath made me free from the law of sin and death.*

Galatians 3:13 *Christ hath redeemed us from the curse of the law, being made a curse for us: for it is written, Cursed is every one that hangeth on a tree.*

Hebrews 2:14 *Forasmuch then as the children are partakers of flesh and blood, he also himself likewise took part of the same; that through death he might destroy him that had the power of death, that is, the devil.*

James 5:14-16 *Is any sick among you? Let him call for the elders of the church; and let them pray over him, anointing him with oil in the name of* *the Lord: and the prayer of faith shall save the sick, and the Lord shall raise him up; and if he have committed sins, they shall be forgiven him. Confess your faults one to another, and pray one for another, that ye may be healed. The effectual fervent prayer of a righteous man availeth much.*

1 Peter 2:24 *Who his own self bare our sins in his own body on the tree, that we, being dead to sins, should live unto righteousness: by whose stripes ye were healed.*

3 John 1:2 *Beloved, I wish above all things that thou mayest prosper and be in health, even as thy soul prospereth.*

For an additional list of healing scriptures, read Dodie Osteen's miraculous testimony of healing from incurable cancer in her book, *Healed of Cancer.*

Authority Over Satan

Isaiah 54:17 *No weapon that is formed against thee shall prosper; and every tongue that shall rise against thee in judgment thou shalt condemn. This is the heritage of the servants of the Lord, and their righteousness is of me, saith the Lord.*

Matthew 10:8 *Heal the sick, cleanse the lepers, raise the dead, cast out devils: freely ye have received, freely give.*

Matthew 18:18 *Verily I say unto you, Whatsoever ye shall bind on earth shall be bound in heaven: and whatsoever ye shall loose on earth shall be loosed in heaven.*

Matthew 28:18 *And Jesus came and spake unto them, saying, All power is given unto me in heaven and in earth.*

Luke 9:1 *Then he called his twelve disciples together, and gave them power and authority over all devils, and to cure diseases.*

Luke 10:19 *Behold, I give unto you power to tread on serpents and scorpions, and over all the power of the enemy: and nothing shall by any means hurt you.*

John 14:12 *Verily, verily, I say unto you, He that believeth on me, the works that I do shall he do also; and greater works than these shall he do; because I go unto my Father.*

John 14:30 *Hereafter I will not talk much with you: for the prince of this world cometh, and hath nothing in me.*

John 17:15 *I pray not that thou shouldest take them out of the world, but that thou shouldest keep them from the evil* [one].

Romans 6:14 *For sin shall not have dominion over you: for ye are not under the law, but under grace.*

Romans 8:37 *Nay, in all these things we are more than conquerors through him that loved us.*

1 Corinthians 15:57 *But thanks be to God, which giveth us the victory through our Lord Jesus Christ.*

2 Corinthians 10:4-5 *(For the weapons of our warfare are not carnal, but mighty through God to the pulling down of strong holds;) casting down imaginations, and every high thing that exalteth itself against the knowledge of God, and bringing into captivity every thought to the obedience of Christ.*

Ephesians 1:3 *Blessed be the God and Father of our Lord Jesus Christ, who hath blessed us with all spiritual blessings in heavenly places in Christ.*

Ephesians 1:19-21 *And what is the exceeding greatness of his power to us-ward who believe, according to the working of his mighty power, which he wrought in Christ, when he raised him from the dead, and set him at his own right hand in the heavenly places, far above all principality, and power, and might, and dominion, and every name that is named, not only in this world, but also in that which is to come.*

Ephesians 4:27 *Neither give place to the devil.*

Ephesians 6:10-17 *Finally, my brethren, be strong in the Lord, and in the power of his might. Put on the whole armour of God, that ye may be able to stand against the wiles of the devil. For we wrestle not against flesh and blood, but against principalities, against powers, against the rulers of the darkness of this world, against spiritual wickedness in high places. Wherefore take unto you the whole armour of God, that ye may be able to withstand in the evil day, and having done all, to stand. Stand therefore, having your loins girt about with truth, and having on the breastplate of righteousness; and your feet shod with the preparation of the gospel of peace; above all, taking the shield of faith, wherewith ye shall be able to quench all the fiery darts of the wicked.*

And take the helmet of salvation, and the sword of the Spirit, which is the word of God.

Colossians 2:10 *And ye are complete in him, which is the head of all principality and power.*

Colossians 2:15 *And having spoiled principalities and powers, he made a shew of them openly, triumphing over them in it.*

2 Timothy 1:7 *For God hath not given us the spirit of fear; but of power, and of love, and of a sound mind.*

James 4:7 *Submit yourselves therefore to God. Resist the devil, and he will flee from you.*

1 Peter 5:8 *Be sober, be vigilant; because your adversary the devil, as a roaring lion, walketh about, seeking whom he may devour.*

1 John 4:4 *Ye are of God, little children, and have overcome them: because greater is he that is in you, than he that is in the world.*

1 John 5:4-5 *For whatsoever is born of God overcometh the world: and this is the victory that overcometh the world, even our faith. Who is he* *that overcometh the world, but he that believeth that Jesus is the Son of God?*

Revelation 12:11 *And they overcame him by the blood of the Lamb, and by the word of their testimony; and they loved not their lives unto the death.*

Revelation 21:7 *He that overcometh shall inherit all things; and I will be his God, and he shall be my son.*

Prosperity

Genesis 13:2 *And Abram was very rich in cattle, in silver, and in gold.*

Leviticus 27:30 *And all the tithe of the land, whether of the seed of the land, or of the fruit of the tree, is the Lord's: it is holy unto the Lord.*

Deuteronomy 8:18 *But thou shalt remember the Lord thy God: for it is he that giveth thee power to get wealth, that he may establish his covenant which he sware unto thy fathers, as it is this day.*

Deuteronomy 28:11-12 *And the Lord shall make thee plenteous in goods, in the fruit of thy body, and in the fruit of thy cattle, and in the fruit* *of thy ground, in the land which the Lord sware unto thy fathers to give thee. The Lord shall open unto thee his good treasure, the heaven to give the rain unto thy land in his season, and to bless all the work of thine hand: and thou shalt lend unto many nations, and thou shalt not borrow.*

Joshua 1:8 *This book of the law shall not depart out of thy mouth; but thou shalt meditate therein day and night, that thou mayest observe to do according to all that is written therein: for then thou shalt make thy way prosperous, and then thou shalt have good success.*

2 Chronicles 26:5 *And as long as he sought the Lord, God made him to prosper.*

Nehemiah 2:20 *Then answered I them, and said unto them, The God of heaven, he will prosper us.*

Psalm 1:2-3 *But his delight is in the law of the Lord; and in his law doth he meditate day and night. And he shall be like a tree planted by the rivers of water, that bringeth forth his fruit in his season; his leaf also shall not wither; and whatsoever he doeth shall prosper.*

Psalm 23:1 *The Lord is my shepherd; I shall not want.*

Psalm 34:8-10 *O taste and see that the Lord is good: blessed is the man that trusteth in him. O fear the Lord, ye his saints: for there is no want to them that fear him. The young lions do lack, and suffer hunger: but they that seek the Lord shall not want any good thing.*

Psalm 35:27 *Let them shout for joy, and be glad, that favour my righteous cause: yea, let them say continually, Let the Lord be magnified, which hath pleasure in the prosperity of his servant.*

Psalm 37:25 *I have been young, and now am old; yet have I not seen the righteous forsaken, nor his seed begging bread.*

Psalm 112:1-3 *Blessed is the man that feareth the Lord, that delighteth greatly in his commandments. His seed shall be mighty upon earth: the generation of the upright shall be blessed. Wealth and riches shall be in his house: and his righteousness endureth forever.*

Psalm 122:7 *Peace be within thy walls, and prosperity within thy palaces.*

Proverbs 10:22 *The blessing of the Lord, it maketh rich, and he addeth no sorrow with it.*

Proverbs 13:22 *A good man leaveth an inheritance to his children's children: and the wealth of the sinner is laid up for the just.*

Joel 2:26 *And ye shall eat in plenty, and be satisfied, and praise the name of the Lord your God, that hath dealt wondrously with you: and my people shall never be ashamed.*

Malachi 3:10 *Bring ye all the tithes into the storehouse, that there may be meat in mine house, and prove me now herewith, saith the Lord of hosts, if I will not open you the windows of heaven, and pour you out a blessing, that there shall not be room enough to receive it.*

Matthew 6:33 *But seek ye first the kingdom of God, and his righteousness; and all these things shall be added unto you.*

Luke 6:38 *Give, and it shall be given unto you; good measure, pressed down, and shaken together, and running over, shall men give into your bosom. For with the same measure that ye mete withal it shall be measured to you again.*

John 10:10 *The thief cometh not, but for to steal, and to kill, and to destroy: I am come that they* *might have life, and that they might have it more abundantly.*

2 Corinthians 9:7-11 *Every man according as he purposeth in his heart, so let him give; not grudgingly, or of necessity: for God loveth a cheerful giver. And God is able to make all grace abound toward you; that ye, always having all sufficiency in all things, may abound to every good work: (As it is written, He hath dispersed abroad; he hath given to the poor: his righteousness remaineth for ever. Now he that ministereth seed to the sower both minister bread for your food, and multiply your seed sown, and increase the fruits of your righteousness;) Being enriched in every thing to all bountifulness, which causeth through us thanksgiving to God.*

Philippians 4:19 *But my God shall supply all your need according to his riches in glory by Christ Jesus.*

3 John 1:2 *Beloved, I wish above all things that thou mayest prosper and be in health, even as thy soul prospereth.*

Victory Over Fear

Exodus 14:13 *And Moses said unto the people, Fear ye not, stand still, and see the salvation of the Lord, which he will show to you to day.*

Joshua 1:9 *Have not I commanded thee? Be strong and of a good courage; be not afraid, neither be thou dismayed: for the Lord thy God is with thee whithersoever thou goest.*

2 Kings 6:16 *And he answered, Fear not: for they that be with us are more than they that be with them.*

Psalm 91:5 *Thou shalt not be afraid for the terror by night; nor for the arrow that flieth by day.*

Psalm 118:6 *The Lord is on my side; I will not fear: what can man do unto me?*

Proverbs 29:25 *The fear of man bringeth a snare: but whoso putteth his trust in the Lord shall be safe.*

Isaiah 35:4 *Say to them that are of a fearful heart, Be strong, fear not: behold, your God will come with vengeance, even God with a recompense; he will come and save you.*

Isaiah 41:10 *Fear thou not; for I am with thee: be not dismayed; for I am thy God: I will strengthen thee; yea, I will help thee; yea, I will uphold thee with the right hand of my righteousness.*

Isaiah 43:1-2 *Fear not: for I have redeemed thee, I have called thee by thy name; thou art mine. When thou passest through the waters, I will be with thee; and through the rivers, they shall not overflow thee: when thou walkest through the fire, thou shalt not be burned; neither shall the flame kindle upon thee.*

Mark 5:36 *As soon as Jesus heard the word that was spoken, he saith unto the ruler of the synagogue, Be not afraid, only believe.*

Luke 1:74 *That he would grant unto us, that we being delivered out of the hand of our enemies might serve him without fear.*

Romans 8:15 *For ye have not received the spirit of bondage again to fear; but ye have received the Spirit of adoption, whereby we cry, Abba, Father.*

2 Timothy 1:7 *For God hath not given us the spirit of fear; but of power, and of love, and of a sound mind.*

Hebrews 13:5-6 *Let your conversation be without covetousness; and be content with such things as ye have: for he hath said, I will never leave thee, nor forsake thee. So that we may boldly say, The Lord is my helper, and I will not fear what man shall do unto me*

1 John 4:18 *There is no fear in love; but perfect love casteth out fear: because fear hath torment. He that feareth is not made perfect in love.*

The Gifts of the Holy Spirit

Isaiah 8:18 *Behold, I and the children whom the Lord hath given me are for signs and for wonders in Israel from the Lord of hosts, which dwelleth in mount Zion.*

Daniel 11:32 *The people that do know their God shall be strong, and do exploits.*

Mark 16:15-18 *And he said unto them, Go ye into all the world, and preach the gospel to every creature. He that believeth and is baptized shall be saved; but he that believeth not shall be damned. And these signs shall follow them that believe; In my name shall they cast out devils; they shall speak with new tongues; They shall take up serpents; and* *if they drink any deadly thing, it shall not hurt them; they shall lay hands on the sick, and they shall recover.*

Acts 1:8 *But ye shall receive power, after that the Holy Ghost is come upon you.*

Acts 2:4 *And they were all filled with the Holy Ghost, and began to speak with other tongues, as the Spirit gave them utterance.*

Acts 8:17 *Then laid they their hands on them, and they received the Holy Ghost.*

Acts 10:38 *How God anointed Jesus of Nazareth with the Holy Ghost and with power: who went about doing good, and healing all that were oppressed of the devil; for God was with him.*

1 Corinthians 3:16 *Know ye not that ye are the temple of God, and that the Spirit of God dwelleth in you?*

1 Corinthians 12:1,4-7 *Now concerning spiritual gifts, brethren, I would not have you ignorant. Now there are diversities of gifts, but the same Spirit. And there are differences of administrations, but the same Lord. And there are* *diversities of operations, but it is the same God which worketh all in all. But the manifestation of the Spirit is given to every man to profit withal.*

1 Corinthians 12:8-11 *For to one is given by the Spirit the word of wisdom; to another the word of knowledge by the same Spirit; to another faith by the same Spirit; to another the gifts of healing by the same Spirit; to another the working of miracles; to another prophecy; to another discerning of spirits; to another divers kinds of tongues; to another the interpretation of tongues: but all these worketh that one and the selfsame Spirit, dividing to every man severally as he will.*

1 Corinthians 14:1 *Follow after charity, and desire spiritual gifts, but rather that ye may prophesy.*

2 Corinthians 10:4 *For the weapons of our warfare are not carnal, but mighty through God to the pulling down of strong holds.*

1 Thessalonians 5:19-20 *Quench not the Spirit. Despise not prophesyings.*

Hebrews 2:4 *God also bearing them witness, both with signs and wonders, and with divers* *miracles, and gifts of the Holy Ghost, according to his own will.*

EIGHT

Claim Your Benefits and Receive Your Inheritance

Now that you have read some of the Will, pray this prayer out loud and lay hold of all God's benefits for you.

"**Dear Heavenly Father, I come boldly to Your throne today to claim my benefits in the kingdom of God. I have an inheritance that You have given me, and I claim it today in the high court of heaven.**

"**I thank You that You so loved me that You gave Your only Son that I might have eternal life. I have the assurance of that eternal life today because the Holy Spirit within me bears witness in my heart that I am Your child.**

"**I thank You that I have received the promise of the Holy Spirit, and I do speak in tongues as the Spirit gives** me utterance. The Holy Spirit gives me continuing power to live a godly life and to be a witness of the Lord Jesus Christ.

"I am healed, and I have been given perfect health, for by Jesus' stripes I was healed and I am healed now.

"I have authority over Satan, and nothing shall by any means hurt me because greater is He that is in me than he that is in the world. I submit myself to God, and as I resist the devil, he must flee!

"I thank You, Father, that today Your Will gives me prosperity. My every need is met according to Your riches in glory by Christ Jesus. As I give, men give unto me. As I seek first the kingdom of God and Your righteousness, all things are added unto me.

"According to Your Will, I am the righteousness of God in Christ. I will not cower under condemnation from the enemy. I will walk in the Spirit, for Christ Jesus has been made unto me righteousness.

"I thank You, Father, that You have not given me a spirit of fear, but of power and of love and of a sound mind. God's perfect love in me and for me casts out all fear in my life. I am free. And whom the Son sets free is free indeed!

"Your Will gives me the weapons of my warfare, which include the gifts of the Holy Spirit. I will desire and earnestly cultivate these gifts of the Spirit that I might edify and build up the body of Christ.

"I thank You, Father, that You have heard my prayer, for I ask it in Jesus' name. You have said that if I ask anything in His name that You will do it. I receive the benefits of Your Will this day with joy and thanksgiving, giving glory to God.

"In Jesus' name, Amen."

BOOKS BY JOHN OSTEEN

A Miracle For Your Marriage
ABC's of Faith
Deception! Recognizing True and False Ministries
How To Claim the Benefits of the Will
How To Demonstrate Satan's Defeat
How To Minister Healing to the Sick
How To Receive Life Eternal
Love & Marriage
Pulling Down Strongholds
Spiritual Food for Victorious Living
The 6th Sense ... Faith
There is a Miracle in Your Mouth

BOOKS BY OTHER AUTHORS

*Healed of Cancer
 by Dodie Osteen

*Overcoming Opposition:
 How To Succeed in Doing the Will of God
 by Lisa Comes

*Six Lies the Devil Uses to Destroy Marriages
 by Lisa Comes

*Also available in Spanish.

Lakewood Church
P.O. Box 23297
Houston Texas 77228